Facts About the Jumping Spider

By Lisa Strattin

© 2023 Lisa Strattin

FREE BOOK

FREE FOR ALL SUBSCRIBERS

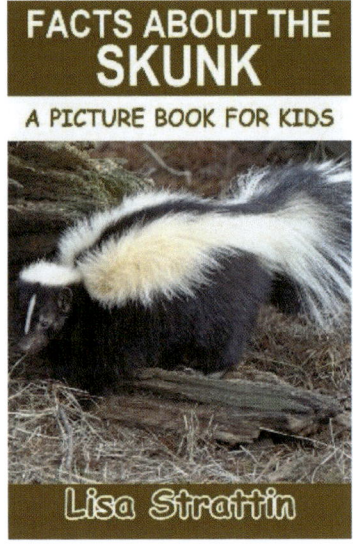

LisaStrattin.com/Subscribe-Here

BOX SET

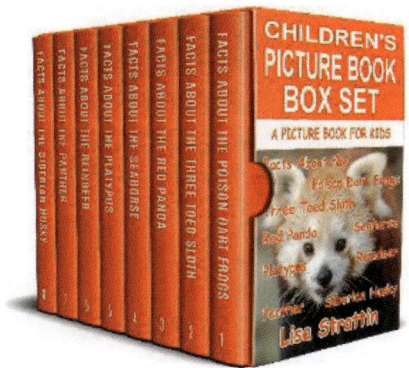

- **FACTS ABOUT THE POISON DART FROGS**
- **FACTS ABOUT THE THREE TOED SLOTH**
  - **FACTS ABOUT THE RED PANDA**
  - **FACTS ABOUT THE SEAHORSE**
  - **FACTS ABOUT THE PLATYPUS**
  - **FACTS ABOUT THE REINDEER**
  - **FACTS ABOUT THE PANTHER**
- **FACTS ABOUT THE SIBERIAN HUSKY**

LisaStrattin.com/BookBundle

Facts for Kids Picture Books by Lisa Strattin

Little Blue Penguin, Vol 92

Chipmunk, Vol 5

Frilled Lizard, Vol 39

Blue and Gold Macaw, Vol 13

Poison Dart Frogs, Vol 50

Blue Tarantula, Vol 115

African Elephants, Vol 8

Amur Leopard, Vol 89

Sabre Tooth Tiger, Vol 167

Baboon, Vol 174

Sign Up for New Release Emails Here

LisaStrattin.com/subscribe-here

All rights reserved. No part of this book may be reproduced by any means whatsoever without the written permission from the author, except brief portions quoted for purpose of review.

All information in this book has been carefully researched and checked for factual accuracy. However, the author and publisher makes no warranty, express or implied, that the information contained herein is appropriate for every individual, situation or purpose and assume no responsibility for errors or omissions. The reader assumes the risk and full responsibility for all actions, and the author will not be held responsible for any loss or damage, whether consequential, incidental, special or otherwise, that may result from the information presented in this book.

All images are free for use or purchased from stock photo sites or royalty free for commercial use.

Some coloring pages might be of the general species due to lack of available images.

I have relied on my own observations as well as many different sources for this book and I have done my best to check facts and give credit where it is due. In the event that any material is used without proper permission, please contact me so that the oversight can be corrected.

⋆⋆COVER IMAGE⋆⋆

https://www.flickr.com/photos/49580580@N02/52255017891/

⋆⋆ADDITIONAL IMAGES⋆⋆

https://www.flickr.com/photos/patrick_k59/25479913448/

https://www.flickr.com/photos/patrick_k59/32016563687/

https://www.flickr.com/photos/49580580@N02/52041442977/

https://www.flickr.com/photos/patrick_k59/51769437310/

https://www.flickr.com/photos/49580580@N02/51116446045/

https://www.flickr.com/photos/119200904@N07/33919082343/

https://www.flickr.com/photos/jean_hort/48879162581/

https://www.flickr.com/photos/patrick_k59/51928667052/

https://www.flickr.com/photos/pamas/34141321873/

https://www.flickr.com/photos/pamas/33626658095/

Contents

INTRODUCTION 9

CHARACTERISTICS 11

APPEARANCE.. 13

LIFE STAGES... 15

LIFE SPAN... 17

SIZE 19

HABITAT 21

DIET 23

FRIENDS AND ENEMIES 25

SUITABILITY AS PETS 27

INTRODUCTION

Jumping Spiders are fascinating little creatures often seen jumping around on plants and walls. They are known for their ability to jump great distances and keen eyesight. They are small, generally less than an inch in length, and can be found in various habitats, including gardens, forests, and even inside homes.

CHARACTERISTICS

The Jumping Spider is a small spider that has eight legs and a body that is divided into two parts: the cephalothorax and the abdomen. The cephalothorax is the front part of the body that contains the spider's head, eyes, and mouthparts. The abdomen is the back part of the body that contains the spider's organs and digestive system.

A significant characteristic of Jumping Spiders is their behavior. Unlike most spiders, which spin webs to catch their prey, Jumping Spiders are active hunters. They use their excellent eyesight to locate and track their prey, and then use their powerful legs to jump on them and subdue them with venom. This behavior makes them highly efficient predators, and they can catch a wide variety of insects and other small prey.

APPEARANCE

The Jumping Spider has a round, compact body covered in short, stiff hairs. Jumping Spider is usually brown, black, or gray and has a distinctive pattern of stripes, spots, or other markings on its body.

A Jumping Spider has eight eyes that are arranged in two rows of four. The front row of eyes is large and can see in color, while the back row is smaller and can see in black and white. Jumping Spider also has two pairs of short, hairy front legs used for jumping and catching prey.

LIFE STAGES

Jumping Spider goes through six main life stages:

1. Egg: Jumping Spiders lay their eggs in silken egg sacs, which they often attach to a leaf or other surface. The eggs hatch after about two weeks.

2. Larva: After hatching, the spiderlings (baby spiders) emerge as small, translucent larvae.

3. Pre-molt: As the spiderlings grow, they enter the premolt stage, stop feeding, and their exoskeleton begins to harden. This stage lasts for about a day.

4. Molt: During the molt stage, the spiderlings shed their old exoskeleton and emerge as slightly larger, more developed spiders. They will molt several times during this stage, which lasts about two weeks.

5. Juvenile: Once the spiderlings have completed their final molt, they enter the juvenile stage. During this stage, they continue to grow and develop, and they begin to hunt and feed on insects.

6. Adult: After about six months, the Jumping Spider reaches adulthood. At this point, it is fully developed and able to mate and reproduce. Adult Jumping Spiders can live for up to two years.

LIFE SPAN

The Jumping Spider has a lifespan of one to two years. This is because they are often preyed upon by other animals, such as birds, lizards, and even other spiders.

However, some Jumping Spiders may live for a little longer if they have plenty of food and good habitat.

SIZE

In terms of size, Jumping Spiders are small, with most adults usually around 1/2 inch in length. This means that Jumping Spider is about the size of a penny.

HABITAT

Jumping Spiders live in various habitats, including forests, gardens, and even inside homes. Jumping Spiders like to live in places with plenty of hiding places, like plants, logs, and rocks. Jumping Spider also likes to live in places with plenty of food, like insects and other very small animals. They are often seen on plants and walls, where they can easily spot food and enemies.

DIET

A Jumping Spider is a carnivore, which means that it eats meat. Jumping Spider's diet consists mainly of insects, like flies, beetles, and moths. Jumping Spiders also eat other small animals, like spiders and caterpillars.

They use their keen eyesight to spot prey and then use their strong front legs to catch and hold onto the prey; after that, they use their fangs to inject venom and paralyze their victim.

FRIENDS AND ENEMIES

Jumping Spiders have a few friends and enemies in the animal kingdom.

Friends

1. Other Jumping Spiders: Jumping Spiders are known to be social creatures and often live in large groups or colonies. They have been observed grooming and helping each other and even sharing food.

2. Other arachnids: Jumping Spiders are not known to be aggressive towards other arachnids and may even coexist in the same habitat.

3. Insects: Jumping Spiders prey on various insects, including flies, mites, and beetles. These insects provide a food source for the Jumping Spider.

Enemies

1. Larger predators: Jumping Spiders are vulnerable to being preyed upon by larger animals such as birds, lizards, and frogs.

2. Pesticides: Jumping Spiders are sensitive to pesticides and can be killed if exposed to high concentrations of them.

3. Human interference: Jumping Spiders can sometimes be seen as pests by humans, leading to the use of bug sprays or other methods of extermination.

SUITABILITY AS PETS

As for suitability as pets, Jumping Spiders can make interesting and low-maintenance pets. They do not require much space or specialized care and are generally easy to feed. However, it is important to remember that they are still spiders and can bite if they feel threatened. For this reason, it is important to handle them carefully and avoid disturbing them unnecessarily.

They can be fed a diet of insects, such as crickets and fruit flies. However, it is important to provide them with a habitat similar to their natural environment and to handle them carefully to avoid damaging their delicate exoskeletons. Because of these requirements, Jumping Spiders may not be the best choice for inexperienced pet owners.

There are many spiders kept as pets. You can visit your local pet store to see if they have a spider you can adopt as a pet (if your parents agree).

COLOR ME

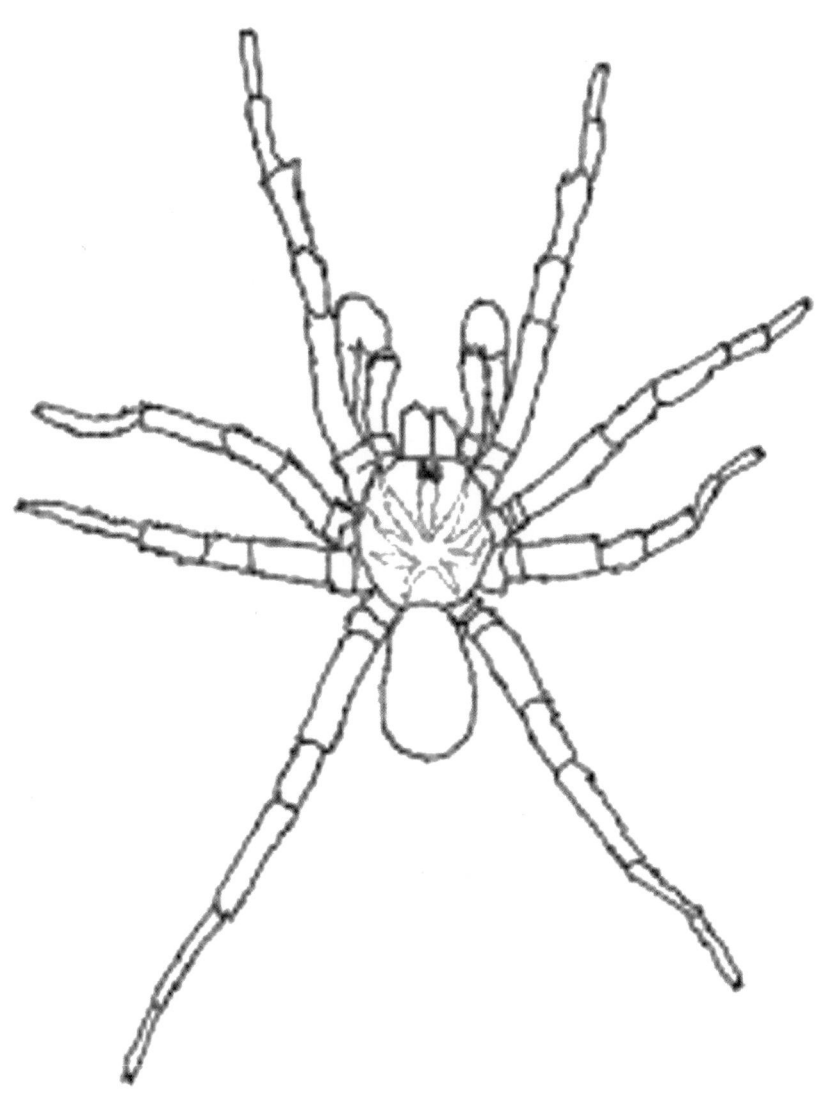

COLOR ME

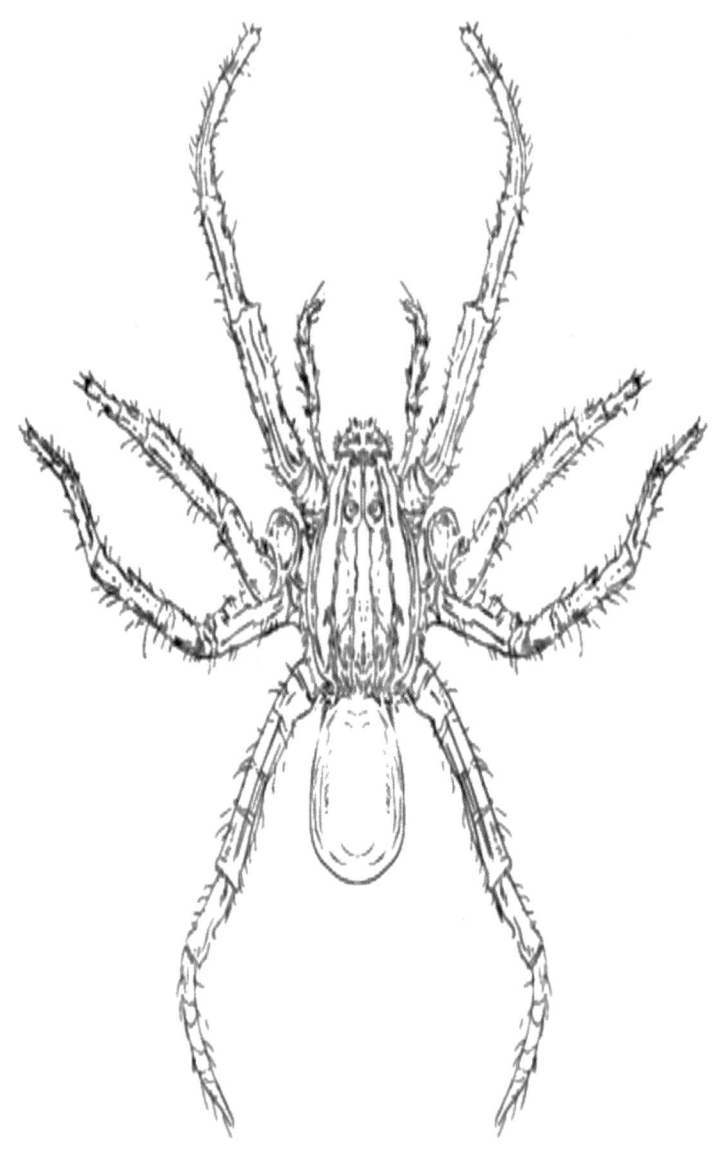

COLOR ME

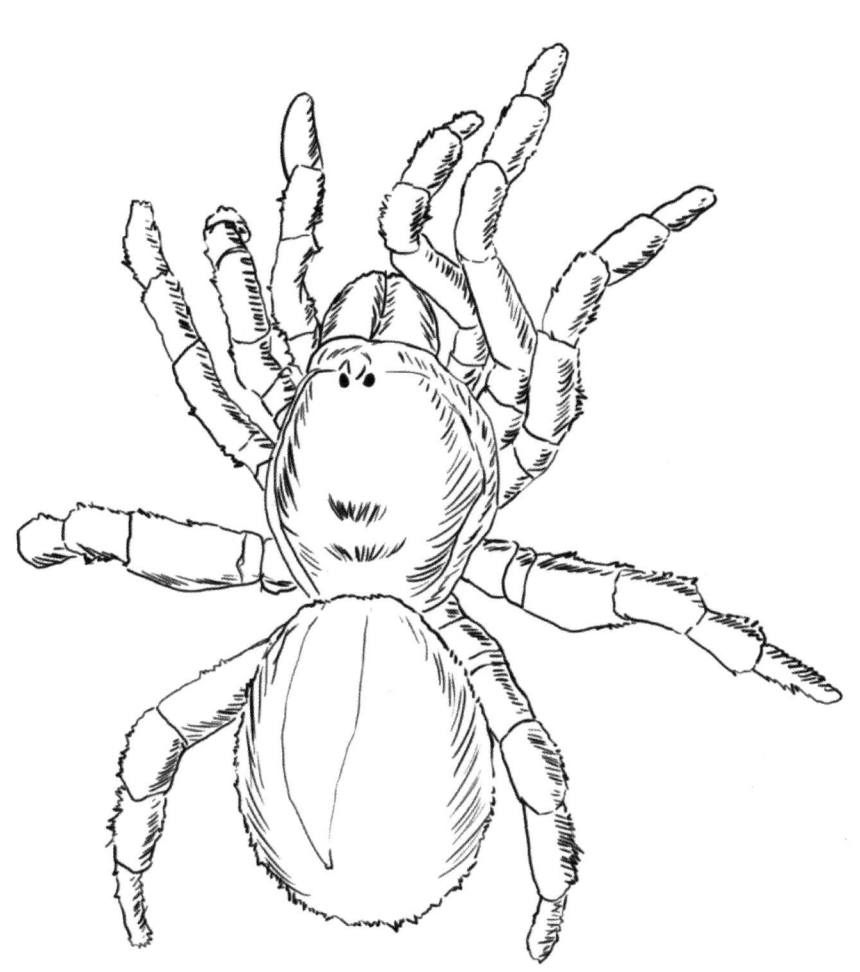

COLOR ME

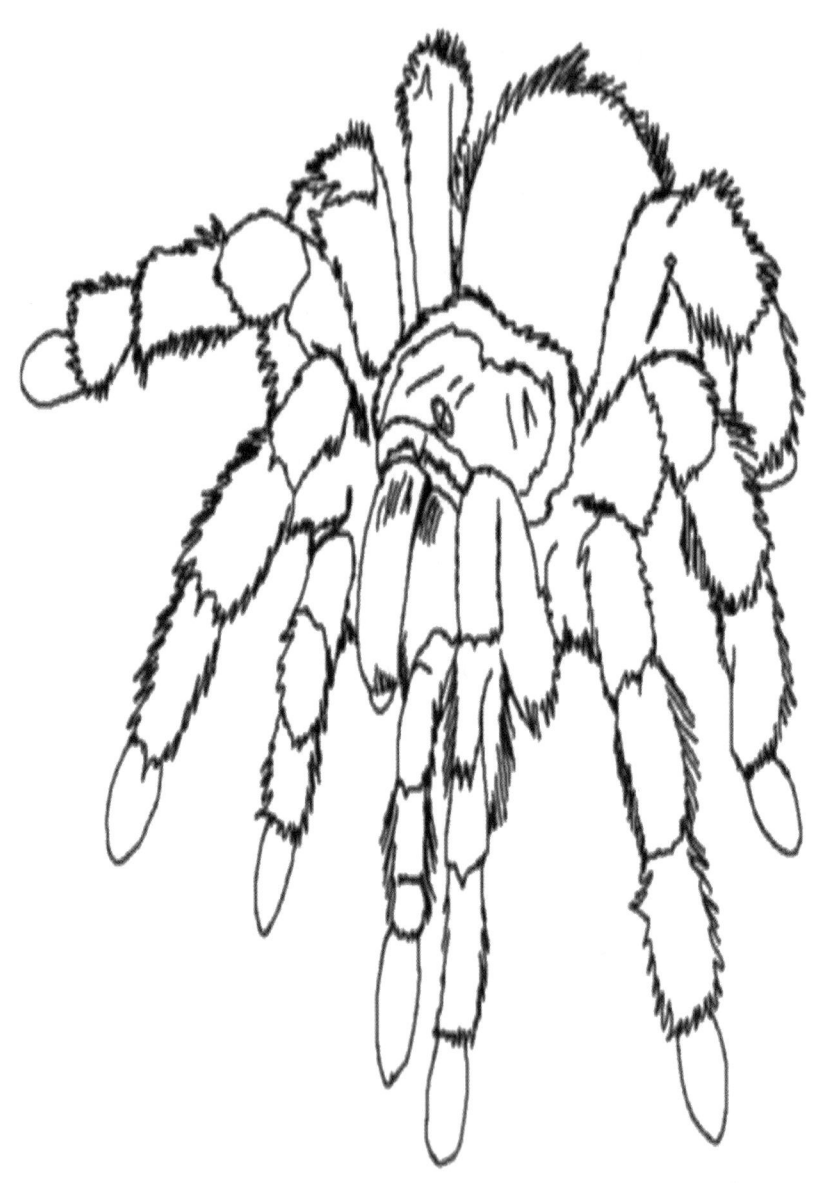

COLOR ME

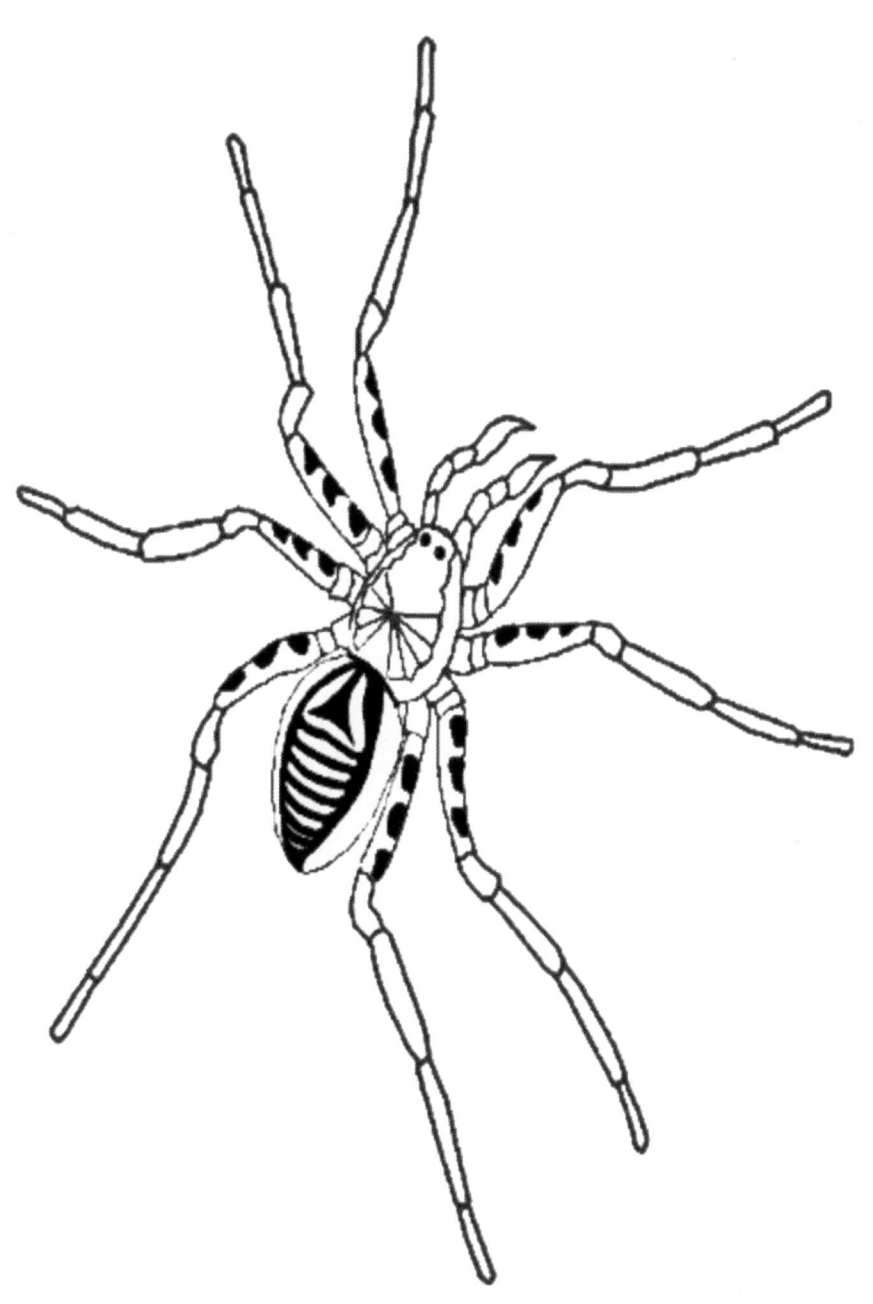

COLOR ME

COLOR ME

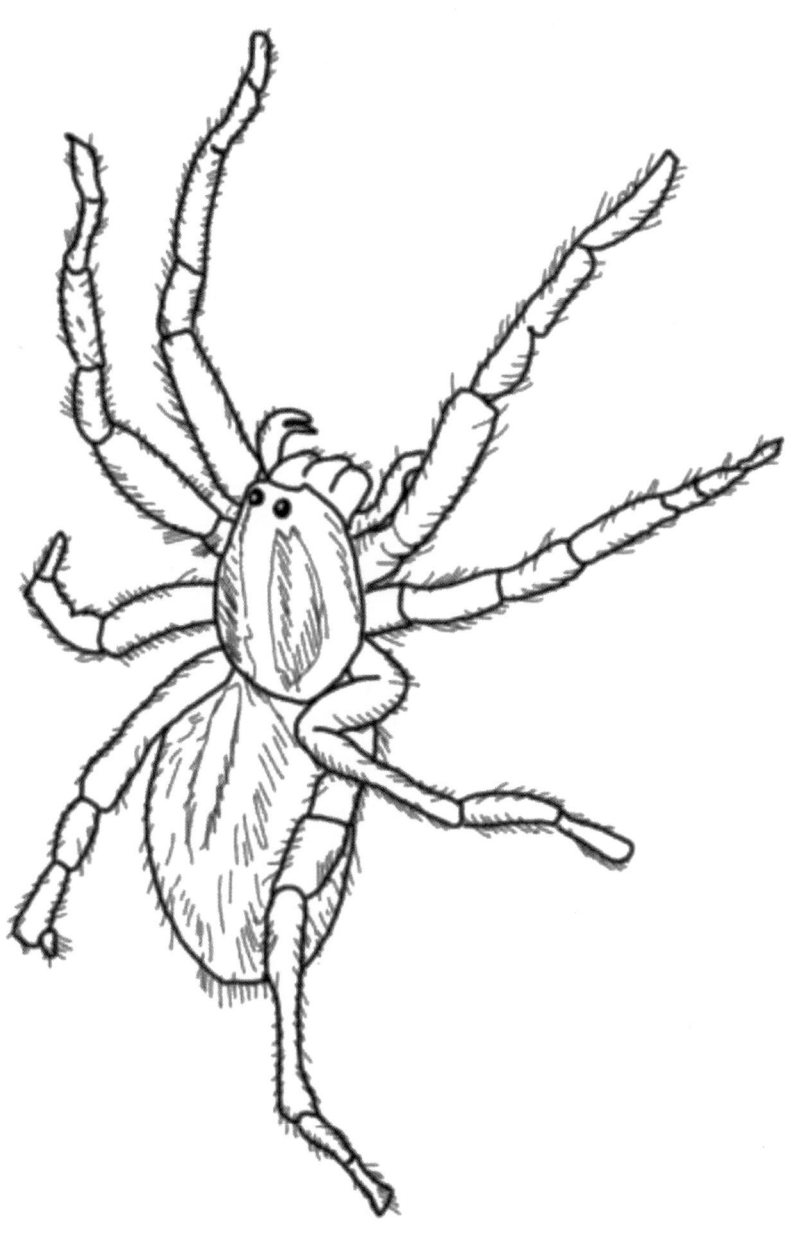

COLOR ME

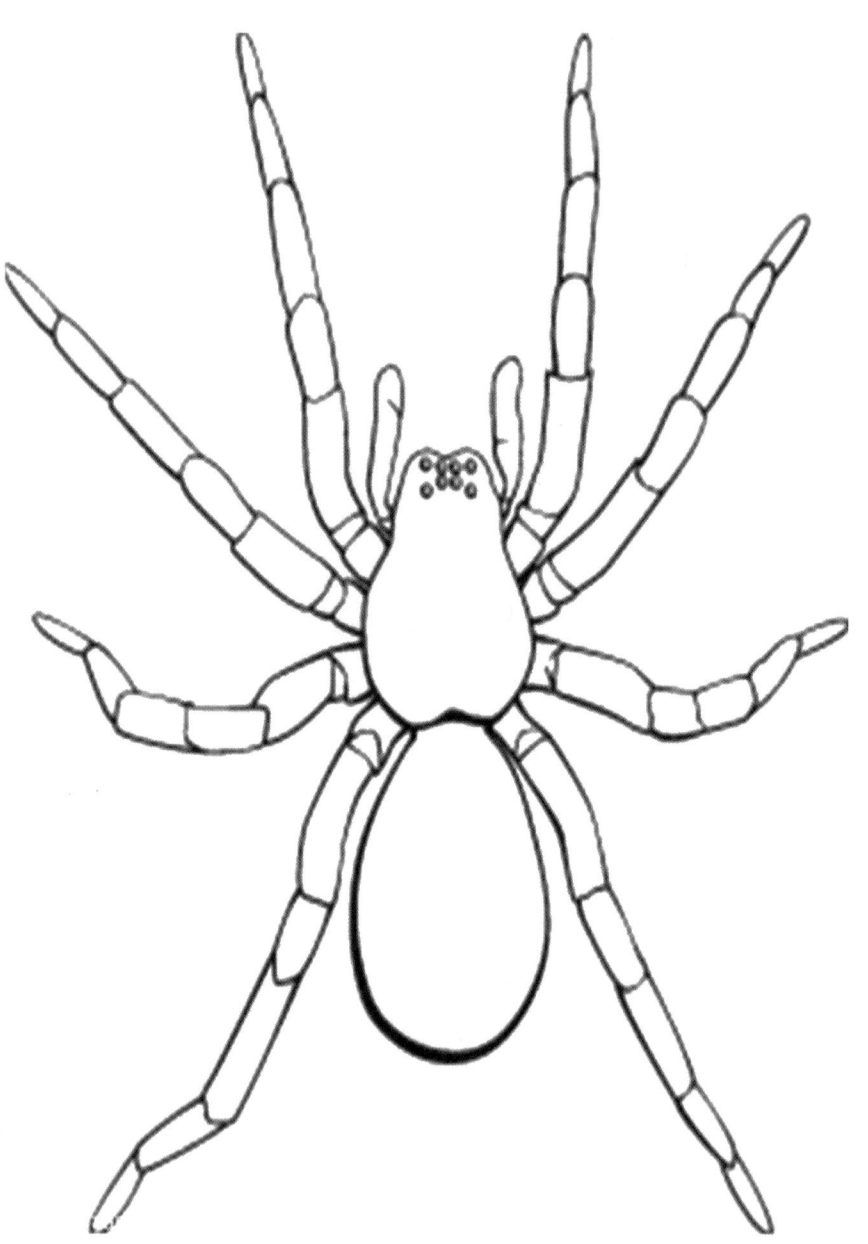

COLOR ME

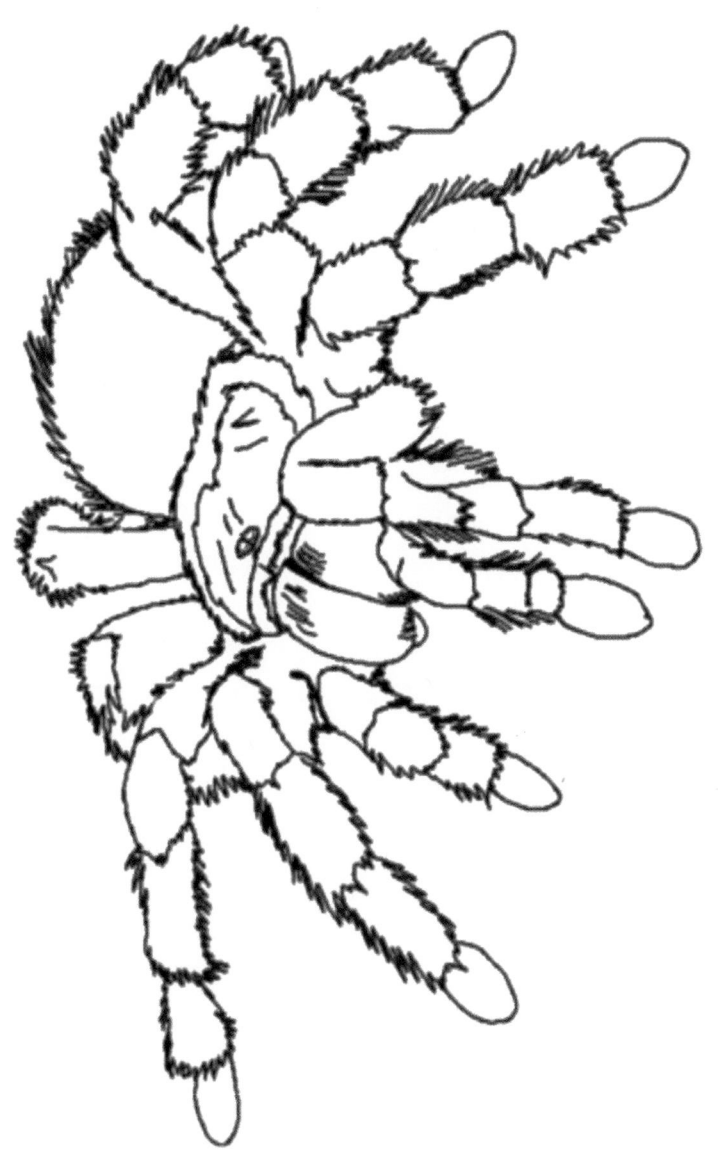

COLOR ME

Please leave me a review here:

LisaStrattin.com/Review-Vol-551

For more Kindle Downloads Visit Lisa Strattin Author Page on Amazon Author Central

amazon.com/author/lisastrattin

To see upcoming titles, visit my website at LisaStrattin.com– most books available on Kindle!

LisaStrattin.com

FREE BOOK

FOR ALL SUBSCRIBERS – SIGN UP NOW

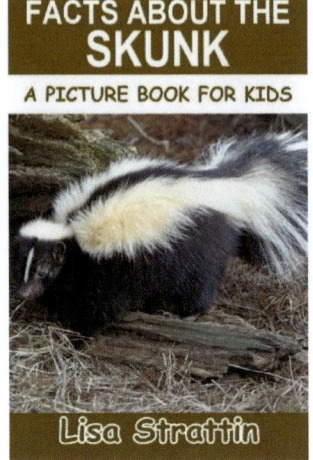

LisaStrattin.com/Subscribe-Here

LisaStrattin.com/Facebook

LisaStrattin.com/Youtube

Printed in Great Britain
by Amazon